God Has Not Forgotten You

Poetry by
Grace J. Mbong

To order additional copies of this book, contact:
Xlibris
844-714-8691
www.Xlibris.com
Orders@Xlibris.com

ISBN: Softcover   978-1-4415-6250-0
           EBook   978-1-6641-8478-7

Print information available on the last page

Rev. date: 07/12/2021

DEDICATION

To my parents: Mr. & Mrs. Mbong Johnny Mbong.

Thank you . . . .

For your encouragements, love and prayers
Being there for me at all times
I would not have made it this far without you
God bless you for all you have done
You are my hero. I love you.

ACNOWLEDGEMENTS:

To my heavenly Father Jesus Christ, thank you so much for the inspiration and the ability you have bestowed upon me to write. Thank you for all you have done for me.

To my mentors: Pastor & Mrs. Issac Okine of Oasis Christian Fellowship, Pastor & Mrs. Rapheal Grant of Eagles Chapel Ministry, Pastor & Mrs. Stallings of Highest Praise Church of God, Pastor Kwame, Pastor Bridget Formiyan and Pastor Ime Ibanga, Pastor Ini Okpon, Clyde Holmes and Pastor Moses Rogers. Thank you so much for your prayers, encouragement words and above all being there when I need strength.

To my siblings: Emmanuel and Joy, thank you for your love and support.
My immediate family: Lillian Mbong, Imoh and Gloria Bassey, Ekanem Mbang, Bobby Effiang, Leo and Mercy Akpan, thank you.
My best friends Osman and Mariama Sesay (Shineshine baby). Having you always by my side is always a blessing. You have always been so wonderful. Thank you so much for your love and support.
To my friends: Victor Ejelonu, Ani Jumbo, Martine Babilla, Romeo Harris, Chrisiana Kumi, Theresa Barnett, Ikepo Talabi, Daniel Menson, Alabaster Choir of Highest Praise Church of God, Oasis Christian Fellowship members, Jericho hour members of Eagles Chapel Ministry, thank you so much.

To my publisher: Thank you so much for your help

Contents

GOD HAS NOT FORGOTTEN YOU

It may look as everything is stagnant,
No way to go, no one to turn to for relieve,
No shoulder to lean on sometimes only a pillow,
That is meant for my sweet dear head.

Comfort for a while but what about tomorrow?
My head is roaming and my head is aching.
Is there any solution to this my problem?
I begin to ask myself a lot of questions.

If your problem is more and heavy than the cross,
More than the problems of Lazarus in the grave.
Look no further, there is a solution.
I remember what the Bible says.

I know the plans I have for you,
Plans to prosper you not to harm you,
Plans to give you hope and a future,
When you seek me with all your heart, you will find me.

God will never leave you nor forsake you,
He is Jehovah, Emmanuel the Sovereign God I am that I am,
His word does not go out and comes back void,
God is not a man that he should lie. God has not forgotten you.

YOUR NIGHT IS ABOUT TO DAWN

Persecutions, tribulations is not for long.
Yes, it is true you may have gone through trials.
Everything you do turns upside down,
You try to climb up the ladder and as you are almost there,
You fall down,
You wait patiently but with no good result.

What do you do in this critical time?
Do you cry, wail or talk about it?
Seek the face of God, leave your problems on
the cross,
Don't stop praying.

Remember weeping endures for a night,
But Joy comes in the morning,
Many are the afflictions of the righteous,
But God shall deliver them from all,
For it is not for long, this time shall pass.

DELAY IS NOT DENIAL

Working hard to survive is not a mystery to me,
Struggling till the wee hours of the morning,
Trying to put all the pieces together,
Is the story I want to say.

We all have struggled sometimes in our
lives,
Where things don't materialize the way
they ought to,
We have been denied because of one thing or
the other,
That drives us crazy to think about it,
Where did I go wrong to be denied of what
I want?

Delay because of certain reasons is not the end of the world for you,
The word "no" is not the final word for victory,
Put the delay in God's hands because he knows it best,
He may not come when you want him to show up,
But be rest assured God is always on time,
Delay is not denial.

BUILT TO LAST

How is your family circle?
Is it built to last or built for destruction?
Is your family torn apart because of strife or selfishness?
Is Commitment a priority in the family?

We all have to spend quality time with our family,
Families are strengthened through doing things together,
Being in God's word also strengthens the family,
Serving others together also unifies the family circle.

Strong families are not just made overnight, they are grown.
We must live in unity with one another,
Work together not against each other,
For we survive storms when we stick together.

WHY ACCEPT MEDIOCRITY?

Why accept average when you are on top?
Why cling to the bottom when you know
that it is not yours?
You are not average, you are above your
circumstances so rise up,
Remember what God says you will be,
that is what you are.

Don't you know that you will make it if you try?
You may have failed but don't give up because you did not succeed.
You can succeed if you are willing to stick to the fight.
Winners do not quit, they persists and try again.

You are brave with wisdom and great potential,
Be bold like a lion and go for your dream,
Do not listen to negative sources all around you,
Average is not your name, you are born for excellence.

YOU CAN MAKE IT

Excellence is achieved through hard work,
Hard work with a lot of patience,
That can be accomplished through perseverance,
If one is willing to go for success.

Don't listen to what people might say when they hear your decision,
Look ahead and focus on your dream,
Take a chance in life and go the extra mile,
The sky is your limit if you want to succeed in life.

WHO IS YOUR FRIEND

We are surrounded in life with a lot of friends,
Wake up! Who is your friend?
Some people come around you to eat you raw,
Make lots of fun, laugh and ridicule you.
Smiles at your face and when you turn around, stabs you at your back,
They look good outside but inside they are devils in disguise.

There is a set of people called good friends,
Through thick or thin, they are always by your side .
When life gets tough, they do not walk away, they stand
by your side,
They do not ridicule you, always willing to accept you for
who you are.

Be careful of who you hang around with,
Some are jealous, speak evil and wish you bad luck,
Some are malicious and think without them you will not
make it in life,
Remember your friend is an attribute of you ,
They are photographs of your future,
Think before you make any one your friend.

TAKE OFF THE MASK

As you look at the mirror everyday,
What do you see?
You see a beautiful image looking back at you,
You might say it is just a shadow,
But it is really you.

Do you like what you see?
If you do not like it, make a change.
You cannot hide behind the mask all day long,
Enjoy the moment,
Love and treat yourself right.

THE PROMISE

The path of life has not been straight,
Full of speed bumps called failure and loops called confusion,
That falls on me like drops of rain,
Which brings tears to my eyes each and every day.

I have been looking for help but no one to turn to,
That could rescue me from all this pain,
I remembered what my parents thought me,
Pray always and put your trust in God.

As years went by, my pains were unbearable,
As I was ready to quit on God, a voice said to me,
I am the Lord, the God of mankind,
Is there anything too hard for me?

Why do you worry about your life?
Who by worrying can add a single hour to his life?
Do not worry about tomorrow,
For tomorrow will worry about itself.

I know the plans I have for you,
Plans to prosper you but not to harm you,
Plans to give you hope and a future,
I will gather you from all the nations and bring you back into exile.

Enlarge the place of your tent,
You will spread to the left and to the right,
Your descendants will dispose nations and settle in their desolate cities,
You will go out in joy and be led forth in peace.

Be strong and of good courage,
Do not let this Book of the Law depart from your mouth,
Do not be afraid, you will not suffer shame,
Do not fear disgrace, you will not be humiliated.

No one else will be able to stand against you all the days of your life,
As I was with Moses so will I be with you.
Hold on to my hand my children,
For I will never leave you nor forsake you,
Never forget the promise.

YOU CANNOT HIDE FROM GOD

We are here in this world to do exploits for God,
What have you done my friend for God?
What are you doing with your time?

Do you know you cannot hide from God?
His eyes are everywhere in this world,
If you hide, he can always find you out.

Where can I go from your spirit?
Where can I flee from your presence?
If I go to the heavens, you are there.
If I make my bed in the depths, you are there.

Be careful of what you do always,
Man might not see you but God sees you.
Remember nothing in all creation is hidden from God,
Everything is uncovered and laid before the eyes of him to whom we must give account.

GET YOUR FIRE BACK

Once upon a time, you had a dream,
Dreams that has not yet come to pass.
You have relaxed may be because of difficulties or uncertainties,
Sometimes you wonder if it is worth trying or not.

Do you know it is one thing to dream and let your dream waste away?
How can a vision get activated when you do not work on it?
As you stand to applaud others when their dreams come to pass,
Don't you think it is about time to be cheered on, too?

You have talents to do what you know best,
God has blessed you with all your five senses.
The fire is in your mind and it needs activation,
Ask God for directions and get your fire back.

BURN UP THE BAD PIECES

How long will you carry problems in your heart?
Problems will lead you to different illness,
That if one is not careful can lead to death,
It could have been prevented if you take precautions.

To forget the past, burn up the bad pieces.
Make no provisions to go back to the dust,
Thank God for the future ahead and always think about it,
The story of life is not finished for you yet.

DON'T LOOK DOWN

Do not look down at yourself,
You are talented, you are blessed,
You are beautiful. You have favor written all over you,
You are special in the sight of God.

Do not beat yourself down because of difficulty,
In times of difficulty, call on God,
He is the answer to your problems,
He is the final resort to your solution,
God has the final say.

DREAM BIG

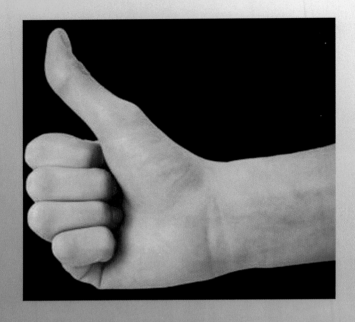

The mind is filled with all sort of thoughts,
Negative thoughts and positive thoughts,
We all dance around the circles each day,
What do I have to listen to?
Is it negative or positive thoughts?

Perhaps someone has spoken
negative words in your life,
May be so called experts has
told you "You will never rise
to the top!"
You are never going to be
successful in life.
Do not listen to these
negative words,
Remember if God is for you
who can be against you.

Program your mind for success by getting rid of negative thoughts,
Set your mind on higher things,
Stop being negative and speak positive to your situation,
Develop a can do altitude at all times,
Even when circumstances don't come your way,
Keep your mind set and dream big.

STAND UP ON THE INSIDE

When adversaries hits on you, you don't have any way to go,
No one to turn to except God,
You have to stand up on the inside.

In the midst of the storm, Praise the Lord,
Don't be a complainer, do not wallow in self pity,
Have a good attitude of a Winner in you.

Do not swift your faith my dear friend,
Do not surrender to the spirit of doubt,
Stand firm and put your trust in God.

THERE IS POWER IN YOU

Look inside of you,
You have greatness in you,
Molded for a specific purpose,
Filled with many unseen miracles.

Break out from your nutshell,
Don't look left or right,
Be determined, get up and look above,
Be confident and take a stand of faith.

Look! Your hands are filled with the blessings of God.
Your head is filled with great wisdom and insights,
To do whatever skill you want to in life.
You can do it because you have the power of God in you.

DO YOU TRUST GOD?

When storms are coming your way,
Everything looks dark and gray,
God can roll the clouds away and make you have a better day,
Do you trust God?

It is okay to say you trust God but do you really do?
Do you lean on God at all times or lean on yourself?
Do you lay your burdens down at the cross?
Or carry it around wherever you go?

When you put your trust in God,
You will never be put to shame.
If you lean on him, he will not let you fall.
If you seek God with all your heart, you
will find him.
Man will fail you but God will never fail,
Put your trust in God and not in man.

NEGATIVITY POISON FOR THE MIND

Do you know that Negativity is like medicine?
When taken in the body, it dissolves,
To do a specific purpose,
To destroy your mind and make you sick.

It is deadly and poisonous,
Eventually things become hard for you,
Life becomes cloudy because you cannot see,
You become bitter because you are frustrated.

Refuse negativity in your life,
You are born for excellence,
You are born to win,
You are created to be a champion in life.

ARE YOUR HANDS CLEAN?

Are you walking in the truth or
walking in the dark?
Is God leading you or are you
leading yourself?
Are you obedient to your calling?
Are your hands clean??

Are you serving others or serving
yourself?
Pretending to be what you know
you are not.
Following after people other than
the spirit of God,
Expecting things to work out
good for you.

We all have to leave our childish toys alone,
Toys are meant for children to play with,
Take inventory of your motives.
Do the right thing and stop acting like a child,
Are your hands clean?

FOCUS ON GOD

Keep your eyes on Jesus Christ,
His messages are words of truth,
Circumstances will always change,
But God never change.
To enjoy this life, one must focus on God.

STORM

The storm of life may come and go,
It may linger for a while with a lot of pain,
It will be frustrating but be patient as you pass through this time,
It shall surely pass.

GRIEVE

Don't grieve when I am gone,
I am around with you my love,
The endless times of this life,
Has surely come to an end for me.

As I fly away like a snow white dove,
Peaceful as could be, relaxing as the sea,
Rejoice because I am going to a beautiful place,
Far beyond the sky, into the heavenly place.

It is peaceful and there is no trouble there,
Full of celebrations and lots of love,
All creations bow down to worship Jesus,
The God of all gods, for there is none like him.

BEHIND CLOSED DOORS

What do you do behind closed doors?
What are you listening to when no one is watching?
Do you do good or do you do evil?
Be careful of what you do
For God is watching you.

LET GOD FIGHT FOR YOU

We all get hurt sometimes in life,
That we let loose and become frustrated,
We feel like doing evil things but a calm sweet voice stops our mission,
Saying "Let go my child. May I, the Lord God Almighty, help you?"

We cannot handle problems that come our way by ourselves,
We might try but fail at the long run,
Before you make a decision in life again,
Consult God Almighty,
Hold your peace and let God fight for you.

TIME

Time, time, time.
There is no time to spare,
I have no time to waste away.
Time is money and precious to me,
So do not waste my time.

Each day has twenty four hours in it,
As you rally around each day,
Do you create time for God your creator?
Do you acknowledge him at all times?

Sometimes you do and sometimes you don't,
You slack, become weary and tired.
You give excuses so as to cover up,
But when it is time for leisure, you are there
and you have time.

In life, it is true that there is no time?
Always remember that you have a creator
who needs you,
More time with God is more time of Joy.
In God's presence, it is always refreshing.

Remember your Creator in the days of your
youth,
Before the days of trouble comes,
And the years approach when you will say,
I have no pleasure in them.

Do not push God to the curve,
As you run all the time to get Money and
Luxuries to enjoy Life,
God is also worth your time.

STAND STILL

When life pushes you back and forth,
You have no place to go, nowhere to hide.
You feel like dying thinking that is the only resort,
Your situation is like you are being held in Prison,
No one to talk to in your darkness hour,
Pray, stand still and see the salvation of the Lord.

LET GO

You think you can make Life without God?
You can't! You will not succeed.
You have no strength. You are so weak.
Let go of pride. Give it all to God.

God will help you when everything fails,
No one can comfort you except Jesus Christ,
Things will change better for you,
If you will let go and let God have his way.

YOU ARE A MIRROR

Working along your busy day every day,
In life, you come across a lot of people.
You smile, talk and share a lot of information with them,
But do you share the good news of God with them?

Do you give a helping hand at all times
Do you show mercy?
Do you love unconditionally or show
love for a reason?
Or react any way you feel like in life?

It is true, by their fruits you will know them?
Your character tells a lot about you.
The examples you show is a mirror that people read and look at,
Know what you do for the world is watching you,
Are you ashamed of being a child of God?

PUSH AND PULL

Push yourself up,
Don't sit and stare.
The journey of life is too long,
There are problems along the highway.

You may be tired yes,
Take a break, relax yourself.
You cannot run away, you have to face trials of life,
The only solution to problems are,
Is to push and pull through.

THE SUN WILL SHINE AGAIN

Look up!
When everything fails,
You have c ome to the end of the rope.
The storm of life is raging,
You have done all you can, stand.

Never forget these words,
Though I walk through the valley of the shadows of death,
I shall fear no evil for you are with me,
Thy rod and staff shall comfort me,
All the days of my life.

One thing I can assure you is,
With God by your side, the sun will shine again.

Do you have dreams you want to fulfill or goals you want to achieve? Author, Grace J. Mbong believes that you have what it takes to make it in life. In this thought provoking anthology, she discovers how each one is born with a special purpose that is uniquely his or hers. Flowing in free verse its messages ring clearly through each word and poetic line challenging you to take action and fulfill the destiny that is sorely yours.

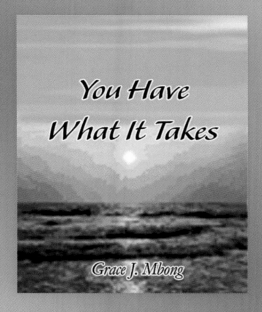

To order additional copies of this book, contact:
Xlibris Corporation
1-888-795-4274
www.Xlibris.com
Orders@Xlibris.com

Printed in the United States
by Baker & Taylor Publisher Services